You Are the Phoenix

By

Lorraine Hardy

ISBN- 9798592254949

Published by Babysteps Publishing Limited 2021

https://babystepspublishing.com
Contact: Kevin A Long

kevin@babystepspublishing.com

BABYSTEPS
Publishing Limited

Disclaimer

Although the author and publisher have made every effort to ensure that the information in this book was correct at press time, the author and publisher do not assume and hereby disclaim any liability to any party for any loss, damage, or disruption caused by errors or omissions, whether such errors or omissions result from negligence, accident, or any other cause.

A CIP copy of this book can be found in the British Library.

TABLE OF CONTENTS

Acknowledgement

To Chris, my husband, my rock and best friend for over 20 years you have stood next to me and held my hand without judgement.

To Booboo and Bear because you truly healed me when I became your mummy.

To Amber my missing bridesmaid

Why I Wrote This Book

Lorraine is one of the worst abused children we have seen here at GOS" (Great Ormond Street).

This was what my adopted mother told me she had been told by Great Ormond Street Hospital when I was 11 years old, that legacy of abuse sat within me for my entire life until I decided that my trauma would not be permitted to control me, my decisions, or my emotions any longer.

I spent the first 5 years of my life living with parents who were abhorrent in their parenting style, sexually abusing me, physically harming me and my brothers, neglecting us all, my biological father spent time in and out of prison and mental institutes, whilst my mother left us with him to protect herself. She is a victim of domestic abuse and has her own trauma from childhood.

I then spent 5 years in foster care, being placed with adoptive parents at the age of 10 without being able to write my own name or read three-letter words.

I spent my later childhood and adolescence fighting my demons. Bulimia, self-harm, drinking, hating myself all whilst trying to be the perfect adopted child. There is no such thing as a perfect adopted child but when you are adopted you spend your time waiting for them to return you to the system, trying to be good enough for them, knowing they opened their home to you when they didn't have to, feeling thankful and obliged.

Through the darkness, I managed to become a social worker and spent twenty years protecting our most vulnerable people in society. Re-living often the trauma of my childhood as I watched what other children went through.

None of this was healthy, I created relationships with unhealthy people, people who would take advantage of me, people I couldn't say no to. Saying no was always so very difficult for me and is still an area of work for me today.

In 2000 I come across NLP, Neuro-Linguistic Programming, and my journey of self-discovery, healing, and thriving began.

For the last 20 years, I have studied NLP, Time Line Therapy, Hypnotherapy, Reiki, Meditation, Quantum Touch, coaching, and counselling. It is through this training that I have become my very own Phoenix, rising from the ashes of the past, entering a new world, where there is joy and love. Self-discovery and evolving are a lifetime of work, but with my personal life experiences, and professional training I am now able to help others find their inner phoenix, and that is where my company You are the Phoenix began. This book is a collaboration of what I have experienced, how I healed, and how together we can work on you becoming your very own phoenix.

But none of this truly explains why I decided to take on this project of writing this book. Ultimately, I did it for two reasons: First, I believe strongly that anyone regardless of their past deserves the opportunity to heal and thrive, and seeing how someone who had my life did make good regardless of all the professionals saying it was impossible. Well, thankfully I don't believe in impossible and I want to share my experience and skills with people who want and need them. Second, I had reached a point in my life in which I wanted to challenge myself. To honour my journey, to get outside my own comfort zone and allow others to see it can be done.

Why Should You Read This Book?

This book is for people wanting to recover holistically from childhood and or adult trauma. Trauma comes in many shapes and colours, and no two traumas are alike. However, this book is written by me, someone who can truly empathise with what living with trauma does to our psyche, relationships, decisions, and behaviours.

This book is not just a self-help book, it is a workbook of compassion, understanding, unconditional friendship, and non-judgemental treatment.

This book looks at the different approaches I found helpful in my journey of becoming the phoenix, and what approaches I use with my clients in their journey of rebuilding themselves, forgiving themselves, loving themselves, honouring their life, and becoming their very own phoenix.

Each chapter will look at a different holistic approach that I use, I will explain how the approach helped me and how I use it with my clients, giving you an insight into the reality of healing, the joy, and the tears, but mainly the truth of possibilities.

I see you; I can feel your pain, I can help you change the pain, I believe in you and your ability to take control. I will hold your hand through the journey and be with you whilst you take each new step. That is what reading this book will do for you.

Chapter 1

What Does Trauma Mean?

Trauma is a reaction to an event that you find highly stressful. That could be being in a war, a natural disaster, an accident, or mistreatment by another. Trauma can cause a wide range of physical and emotional symptoms.

Some people who experience a traumatic event do not develop an adverse effect, but many do. Some have an emotional effect for a short period of time whilst others have more long-lasting effects.

I was affected long term emotionally by the experiences of my traumatic childhood.

I am a victim of sexual abuse at the hands of my biological parents, I witnessed domestic violence, and was neglected. I was never permitted to be a small child, Santa never existed, and by the age of five I had been removed twice and then given back to my biological parents, I had three brothers all younger that I tried to protect and look after. My biological mother had left us all in the care of him, the monster that is my biological father, because she decided to look after herself rather than the four children that she had brought into the world. She just left, leaving me to be the mother, the caregiver, I was five. She chose herself, she left us behind like we were rubbish and unimportant.

At the age of five and a half, we were all removed permanently from my biological parents, back then the professionals didn't consider the trauma of separating siblings, we were separated to never know one another again. Not only did I lose the only parents I knew, but I also lost my brothers who I loved. I lost myself.

I was one of the lucky ones in care, I went to live with a wonderful foster family, I stayed with them for five years until it was deemed, I was ready for adoption. Yet again I was removed without my consent from the people I loved, by the age of 10 I had lost two sets of parents and 8 siblings, plus the extra siblings my biological parents had then had whilst we were in the care system who I have yet to ever meet or even know their names.

I went to live with my adoptive parents at the age of 10, being placed with no contact with my brothers being permitted. The grief that I felt was all-consuming, but I was being told I had to be happy, I had been chosen for adoption. That action alone I was left believing should be enough for me to be happy.

The long-term effects of this have included emotional, physical, and psychological conditions on me. The experience of abuse on an individual regardless of gender or age can and does have devasting effects on every aspect of our lives, on our body, behaviour, thoughts, and emotions. The reality for me like many is that life was a struggle, being happy was difficult, and I felt invisible.

It's perfectly usual and acceptable to feel the effects of trauma. I often have clients who try to hide their feelings or not talk about how they feel because they believe people don't want to hear, and maybe don't know how to listen or understand.

When Gary a client of mine first came to see me, some of the most important things he said was that he felt other people were embarrassed by his trauma. He felt he should have come to terms with what had happened to him already and felt as a man he should be stronger. There were many 'should's' in that initial meeting. He felt he didn't have the right to his emotions, he wasn't allowed to be upset with what had happened to him, he felt his family didn't want to hear what he had to say, he felt he needed to hide, he felt invisible. That caused Gary to self-medicate with alcohol and drugs.

Some of my clients have experienced a whole heap of different feelings whilst others have experienced less. There is no 'normal' because being abused, hurt, or experiencing a traumatic event is not 'normal'

I spent so many years feeling, guilt, shame, embarrassment that people might think differently about me, I would have outbursts of anger or sudden sadness, I can and have felt lonely even when surrounded by people. Even when I started therapy, I went through periods of feeling numb, confused, vulnerable, and in denial. All of these feelings were mine, and I now accept them. My past is part of who I am today, my reaction to my past is what makes me who I am today. I try to help my clients accept their reactions and feelings. The first step of recovery in my experience is acceptance, knowing that you are not to blame, and what you have experienced is not OK but that you can and will be OK regardless of it.

Many people suffer from PTSD (Post-traumatic stress disorder). This is a disorder caused by highly stressful events, often frightening. My clients who have PTSD will relive the event, through nightmares and flashbacks. I remember when I started my recovery, I would have nightmares so bad that I tried to force myself to stay awake. I would drink copious amounts of red bull, caffeine pills anything to stop me from sleeping. That in its self-made me more unwell, it affected my ability to mentally function. It made me question whether recovery was what I wanted, it seemed so hard, and felt like an impossible journey.

The problem with choosing not to recover, and having PTSD means you spend your life often having depressive moments, anxiety, myself and many others spend days and sometimes longer being totally dissociated, nightmares continue, which cause sleep problems, difficulties concentrating, and sometimes suicidal thoughts.

When you break all that down, all those feelings, behaviours, reactions to something we had no control over happening to us, seems terribly unfair, it's disgraceful that a human being has to go through such emotional turmoil, that is why I created You are the Phoenix. I believe we all, victims of trauma deserve to be healed, and I believe we can all heal to some level, a level that allows us to feel and experience joy.

Certainly, some people become very unwell, they may abuse alcohol, drugs, self-harm, they may have psychotic episodes, develop personality disorders, have problems with relationships, and struggle to be parents.

In my 20 years of being a social worker, I rarely met a parent who was struggling with their parenting who had not had some trauma in their lives.

It's a cycle, that without proper holistic intervention just continues generation after generation. When I first studied social work, I remember being told that abused people become abusers. Well yes sometimes this can be true, but not always, I am so passionate about changing the stereotype, changing the noise about traumatised people, we can be successful, we can be great parents, we can be loved unconditionally. We are not untouchables, we are not lepers, we are just human beings who had had events happen to us that were unfair, unjust but that is our journey to embrace.

With the right treatment, people can address the root cause of the trauma and find constructive ways to manage their symptoms.

Gary was unsure whether he was ready to recover from his abuse, he had been so used to the abused Gary he felt that recovery might change him. Here is the secret, it does change us, recovery changes the way we look at our lives and the events that have affected us.

Gary was suffering from severe anxiety and would often in sessions have panic attacks, his body was stuck in the past and he found living in the present difficult. He would often say to me he was going mad; he wasn't, he just couldn't control his reactions to his experiences.

Working with the systems he was experiencing and finding ways of managing them became beneficial. In time he came to understand the triggers of his trauma. We would revisit the negative experiences and he would gain a sense of ownership over them; he began to move beyond the trauma of just survival to actually living.

Working with a person who has experienced trauma is a complex issue, it's important that I have a good understanding of empathy, show unconditional regard, and respect. I always try to create an environment of hope and empowerment.

Recovery in my experience is a collaborative effort between me and my client, I always respect the pace of our sessions on what the client can manage and use many different holistic approaches to best suit the individual.

When I started my recovery feeling secure in any of the work, I was undertaking was pivotal, which is so important for anyone choosing to heal from trauma.

My experience of learning to come to terms with my past was to consider less conventional approaches to healing. Going into therapy wasn't right for me, I tried several times, and that's why I started to look for alternative methods, holistic approaches to change and heal.

I found approaches that were best for me in managing my problems and issues. Utilising a number of strategies and techniques from Reiki to Coaching. I wanted to work on myself creatively, without focusing on the actual events. That's when I initially came across Neuro-Linguistic Programming, which sent me in the direction of hypnotherapy, timeline therapy, and meridian therapy. From there I learnt more about healing the spirit, not just the body and mind, which took me on a journey of discovery. Reiki, Quantum Touch, and Hands-on Healing. Later I found Coaching and realised that I had got something out of each of these approaches which have helped me become the person I am now.

The training I have undertaken and the insight into the human condition that I have because of my experiences have led me to be often a rock for friends who go through sudden trauma. I do not shy away from people who are experiencing pain, I do not feel uncomfortable around those suffering. My life as painful as it has been had made me an incredible human being with deep compassion for people and this, I am proud of. No suffering is worse than any other, we all have a path to walk, we all have a part to play on the main stage, and I play my part with pride. If it wasn't for the heartache and pain I suffered I would not have the strength of a lioness.

It is with 20 years of self-discovery, self-healing, and training that I embark on supporting others in their journey of becoming their very own phoenix. I get to know you as the individual, the trauma you have experienced, and build a bespoke approach to your own journey.

Many people come to me, thinking they have to go over all their traumatic events, they don't. Sometimes we discuss bits, but my approach is that focusing on the person and their needs are what is important. I have found that telling the story of the trauma is ineffective in bringing any relief from the effects of the trauma. Also talking about the event when the time isn't right can be harmful and retraumatizing for the individual.

We begin working together by not focusing on the trauma story itself. I found in my recovery that focusing on the story added to the injury and pain. We start our early sessions on restoring a sense of safety, we find how you self-regulate. Those who have experienced trauma are often overly alert and creating a reduction in that alertness allows the person to discover a strengthened awareness for coping with stress. It's that preparation that then allows for considering strategies that directly deal with the trauma story. This is to stop any traumatisation.

My framework provides such a complex, whole-person approach by designing a trauma treatment programme that is as unique as the individual. What is important to me is that the person's well-being is the focus, their emotional, physical, cognitive, spiritual, and social needs are achieved in the long run.

I am mindful that many people embark on therapy for trauma because they are experiencing pain as a result of the trauma. Trauma is pain, pain is part of our lives and we have to come to terms with that. What's important to recognise and understand is that any trauma work we may do, may not result in the pain disappearing. What changes is that the trauma no longer dominates your life. The trauma and any pain relating to it become but just one part of your life.

Chapter 2

How Does Trauma Affect the Adolescent?

During my teenage years, life became increasingly more difficult. I always stood out in school, when I went to my new primary school after being placed for adoption, I arrived halfway through the year as the newly adopted child who was unable to read or write. A small village where everyone knows everything about you, I knew people spoke about me, I was that child who people were friends with because they felt sorry for me. I hated school, my behaviour regressed, I presented as a child much younger, I was non-compliant, oppositional, and aggressive at times.

As I was unable to read or write being at school was such a challenge. Concentrating and listening was hard, I was so preoccupied with my move and the new family I was now part of that my inattention was often misunderstood. I wasn't an easy child to be friends with I know, I didn't understand the classroom norms, social networking was a foreign language to me, I would often lie hoping to sound more interesting I was hypersensitive and hypervigilant, which meant keeping friends was difficult.

Through all of that though I did start to read and write, nowhere near enough to pass the 11+ so when it came to secondary school, I went to the school where my mother was a very strict deputy headteacher of A large London borough school, It was not an easy ride for sure.

I was bullied, I continued to stand out, this time because of the position my mother held within the school, therefore making friends was really difficult. I knew inside I was damaged I am convinced people knew and picked up on that stuff, I was needy, desperate to fit in, I just wanted to be normal, and find a group of people I could call my own. I would take anybody, if they would take me, I just wanted to be liked. Trying so hard to fit in and be normal was impossible and therefore my coping mechanism was bulimia. My eating disorder began when I was 14, bulimia, and self-harm became my daily ritual.

Bulimia is a mental health disorder; it can affect anyone of any age or gender. Bulimia is when someone is caught in a cycle of eating large amounts of food, often called bingeing, and then throwing up. Sometimes it can include taking laxatives, or excessive exercising.

I just ate and threw up; I didn't do excessive exercise or take laxatives. It gave me control of my body, my thoughts, and my life. I'm not sure about other sufferers of eating disorders, but although I no longer throw up, the feelings of food control have never left me.

I have had many clients who in their adultescents had eating disorders, Sarah came to me as a 39-year-old woman who had been in and out of mental health clinics her whole life and been on many different types of medication. A whole lifetime of feeling unwell, never really knowing what tomorrow would bring, or whether she even wanted to wake up tomorrow. Her eating disorder had come and gone throughout her life and she was now at a time where she felt ready to conquer the disorder. Sarah was a victim of incest and used her disorder to control her emotions and she believed that not eating allowed her to concentrate on that rather than remembering her past, as a young adult when her disorder started, she didn't get the treatment and care that was required which is why even today she struggles.

I was classic in my reasoning for being bulimic, it was the way I coped with difficult emotions, just like Sarah, it helped me manage my upset and anger. I felt totally out of control in everyday life, I couldn't understand my insides and how I felt. I did have control over the speed at which I would eat and then the purge.

The key for adultescents is getting help sooner rather than later, recognising there is a problem, and getting the right treatment. The result of not getting treatment young is a lifetime of consequences.

At 14, I started to spiral inside out of control. I started to have sex, self-harm, I started to drink, smoke and I found my birth mother. Whilst keeping all of this information and behaviours are hidden from the people in my life. There was deep darkness right at the pit of my soul, that no one was able to see but I was able to feel. This cumulated in a suicide attempt whilst at school.

I did start to attend an eating disorder clinic for therapeutic support when I was 14 and whilst talking about my adoptive parents and home life the counsellor began to question some of my mother's parenting techniques. This was a big mistake, my mother removed me from the clinic and therefore all support for my eating disorder ended. I was left stranded with a fully grown disorder, a completely out of control mental illness with nowhere to turn.

I do not believe that blame is healthy for anyone's recovery, and forgiveness is needed if we are to thrive post any trauma. I do not blame the decision my adoptive mother made, but I can acknowledge that that decision was unhelpful in my recovery, as it prolonged my recovery.

Self-harm is a particularly adolescent phenomenon, it can affect all groups but most studies have shown the peak in mid-adolescence. For many teenagers, self-harm can help cope with difficult feelings and a way to release tension and stress. The pain from hurting one's self can feel like a distraction from the emotional pain inside.

I used to cut my arms as a way of shutting out the pain in my soul. I felt so lost and empty. The people around me all felt that I should be super happy and content, but I didn't feel that way. I felt consumed by the level of sadness I felt, the number of people who had been removed from my life was unbearable. Finding my birth mother did not help, she showed no insight into her behaviour, and to this date has never said sorry. Part of my recovery was in fact to remove her from my life which I will discuss in more detail in a later chapter. Sometimes the decisions we need to make, to heal ourselves are very difficult and emotionally distressing.

Going back to the self-harming, this followed me into my early twenties, not until I found NLP and timeline therapy did, I recover from this behaviour. Again, something I will discuss further in a later chapter.

When caregivers come to me regarding their children and needing support, I tell them the story of me being removed form therapy because its important to know, as caregivers of children sometimes we make mistakes in our decisions, we are consumed by our own demons and flaws that a simple comment from a therapist cannot be the reason the child does not get the help required. Sometimes when in recovery we hear things that are difficult to digest, we may feel guilty as caregivers and not ready to accept our part but nothing we feel can ever be on par with what a child who has experienced trauma feels.

I now know that all that I was feeling and going through are typical behaviours and reactions to childhood trauma.

The possibilities are endless when it comes to the effect's childhood trauma can have on an adolescent's development, not only are the possibilities endless they can also be very complex. Emotional abuse, neglect, sexual abuse, physical abuse, witnessing domestic violence, etc., can all interfere with a growing child's psychological, social, and emotional development (Cook, Spinazzola, Ford, Lanktree, Blaustein, Cloitre, & Van der Kolk, 2005).

Adolescents who experience a traumatic event are often consumed by these strong emotions. Caregivers need to understand the ways a child and or a young adult manage distress and trauma so that they can get the right support.

A young person handles trauma differently to younger children or adults. A small child is reliant on family, whereas adolescents look to their peers and friends, for caregivers to help young adults they must understand the ways the young person manages distress.

A decline in mood typically accompanies a teenager who has experienced trauma. Sadness and anger are more prevalent, this will be a direct result of the trauma.

There is often an increase in conflict at home, parents and caregivers are unaware of what is going on in their child's mind, and may attribute moodiness as a typical growing teenager, whilst this can be true, it is important to keep in mind symptoms related to trauma.

Teenagers have higher academic demands placed upon them, increasing their stressors. A traumatised teenager will likely experience a decline in grades and overall performance in areas that they typically performed well in.

Having the memories of the trauma is suffocating and all-consuming therefore their ability to concentrate declines because intrusive and unwanted thoughts replay in their mind.

The transition from being a child to a teenager can be difficult without any trauma in one's life. Young adults can often lose their confidence that they once had when younger, teenagers become aware that they are less dependent on their family and can make it 'on their own'

A key thing for caregivers to remember is that friends and peer groups are often the most important thing for a teenager. Adolescents get a sense of their normality from their friends and peers, a traumatised adolescent will seesaw between independence and insecurity which can be contradictory behaviour and confusing not only to the young person but to the caregiver also.

I am not one to usually list a load of symptoms, however in this case it's important to have an awareness of what to look out for.

Every young person is different, but common symptoms of distress include:

- Strong emotions such as sadness, anger, anxiety, and guilt.
- Overreacting to minor irritations.
- Repetitively thinking about the traumatic event and talking about it often.
- Disturbed sleeping patterns.
- Withdrawing from family and friends.
- Wanting to spend more time alone.
- Being very protective of family and friends.
- Returning to younger ways of behaving including giving up responsibilities or a sudden return to rebellious behaviour.
- Increased need for independence.
- Self-absorption and caring only about what is immediately important .
- Loss of interest in school, friends, hobbies, and life in general .
- A pessimistic outlook on life, being cynical and distrusting of others.
- Depression and feelings of hopelessness.
- Difficulties with short-term memory, concentration, and problem-solving.

Being a social worker who specialised in childhood abuse, I quickly realised I was more 'normal' and typical than I could have imagined. It gave me a sense of acceptance of how I acted out as a teenager. Nothing I did was unexpected to the trained eye, but that also infuriated me. I hated being a statistic, an expected person, doing what the books said I would do, when really if I had been given all the right help, tools and treatment much earlier in my life maybe I would not have been a statistic. Maybe I would not have been drinking at 14, having sex, or smoking, I needed to do other traumatised children coping strategies.

Working with children and young adults for two decades who are or have experienced trauma I have seen first-hand how family problems can occur after the event.

Families don't talk about what happened, the family can often misunderstand a teenager's behaviour, the teenager may be seen as being difficult, parents and caregivers can get hurt when they see their child prefer to talk to their friends over them and family members argue of what points of view.

There are a number of strategies that can be put in place to help your teenager feel and react differently. I encourage the family to communicate without judging or advising the young person until they ask for feedback. Families need to show that they really care for their children and are genuinely interested in their wellbeing. Sometimes it's helpful to make changes to responsibilities during recovery, being flexible and not sticking to how things were before the event are crucial. Give and support even when it feels impossible and extremely difficult.

I have found from my personal and professional experience that a peer network is crucial for recovery. The young person's friends can support their recovery by listening. Trust is often difficult for a person who has experienced trauma, creating a space that feels safe, and non-intrusive can be helpful. I have had the same best friend since I was 14, we are still best friends to this day, and she is probably the person who saw me at my worst and still loved me unconditionally, and for that, I owe her so much, that she could never imagine. Michelle, I thank you for the deepest part of my soul. I was lucky, a lot of young adults do not find a person with who they can connect to and be totally honest with. When I am working with teenagers, this is a crucial part of their recovery, finding that person who can be theirs.

Also having a safe space at home, allowing the young person to know they can share anything with you or someone else within the network and that they will be listened to without judgement and or punishment. Adolescents often don't share their trauma especially if the trauma relates to sexual, physical, neglect, or domestic abuse, but knowing you are there for them is the key.

Finding the right treatment is important from as early as possible, whilst talking therapies have their place, alternative methods are a cornerstone for trauma recovery. Later in this book, we will go through some of those alternative approaches and how they can help.

Chapter 3

How Does Trauma Affect the Adult?

Being an adult usually means you have got your shit together, well that is not the case for so many people including myself.

There is no way of hiding from it, if you experienced trauma as a child or young adult or had a traumatic event happen in adulthood you will show signs of that trauma.

Children make meaning out what happens to them and around them and create an internal map of the world from that, which helps them cope. If children don't create a new internal map as they grow up, their old ways of seeing the world will damage their ability to function as adults.

As someone who specialises in working with traumatised adults and being one myself, I see how they carry the emotional wounds with them into adulthood. They often create a false self.

What I have learnt whilst walking this very long path, is that when children are hurt and not protected by their parents, they try to become the child they think their parents will want. This results in feelings being buried so that their needs in some way can be met, therefore creating a false self, the person the outside world sees.

When we hide our feelings and emotions, we lose touch with who we really are. We must remember that our feelings are an integral part of us, hiding these feelings is a way of protecting ourselves from being further hurt but doesn't actually allow us to be truly seen.

I spend much of my professional time helping people uncover their authentic self, by allowing them to reconnect with their feelings and express the emotions they need and want to.

I find this fascinating, although many of my clients enjoy the outcome of this work, and like being their authentic self, my experience is that they continue to hide their true self from many people. I do this also. The number of people who have said to me, "you don't seem to be someone who comes from a troubled past" well of course I don't seem that to you, why would I allow you to see that. What I have learnt on my journey is that there is no perfection or complete rebuilding of ourselves, what happens is an acceptance of some things, a realisation of others, and an ability to not have the negative emotions that we once did control us. Healing and recovering does not remove what happened to any of us, he just releases the horridness and impact on us.

What we believe about ourselves is what creates and feeds our self-talk. How we talk to ourselves can disempower us completely. Negative talk makes us have little control over our lives, continuing to be the victim. Reiki and other energy healing have helped me with this, and the word victim is almost a swear word for me. It triggers negative self-talk for me, but I now know that and can support me when needed. The reality is whether I like it or not, I was a victim, and being ashamed of that word does nothing but give my abusers control over me which I refuse to do. Sometimes when my self-talk gets bad I go out into a field and shout the word VICTIM really loud. I almost certainly look like a madwoman but whatever gets you through the day right?

My clients do not want to be victims, they want to be thrivers and survivors. Language is a funny thing because for some even the word survivor is incredibly difficult. I used to work with a lady who had, had a terrible upbringing and many things happened to her which were horrendous, she had achieved so much regardless of her past and I used the word survivor and she was incredulous with me. The word survivor meant to her that she was a victim, that is something she refused to have assigned to herself. I am now always led by my client, using the terminology that they are comfortable with. Regardless of terminology what I attain for my clients is for them to no longer feel like a victim, but to feel as if they have concurred with what happened to them.

Having a choice is what's important, of course, we had no control or choice over the trauma, but as adults, we have the choice on how we will manage the results, and change is possible.

When I see clients, sometimes they cannot express anger, this is because they have suppressed their emotions. That doesn't mean they don't feel anger or get angry, they don't know how to express it. Without learning how to express anger and other emotions, you then can't move beyond that emotion. You must acknowledge your emotion and understanding what the trigger for it is, otherwise, you will stay paralysed by the emotion.

For adults who experienced neglect and or abandonment, as adults, they bury the emotions and fear in the hope that you will not be abandoned again. When we don't allow ourselves to feel our feelings, we end up being passive which results in us not living our life to its potential.

Burying feelings results in us burying ourselves. Because of trauma, adults learn to hide parts of themselves, which for a while may have been helpful, but for recovery, we need our feelings to tell us who we are and what we are and then it leads us to become the people we want to be.

I have as previously said suffered the loss of many people in my life, and this is an area I work closely in with clients. Professionally I have worked with parents who have lost children, and this is very close to home for me as I have also had friends who have lost children as well myself suffering many miscarriages.

After a loss, the brain releases chemicals which like in any other trauma-based event, we "fight, flight or freeze" I have seen each response and experienced each response. The pathways within our brain we rely on for most of our lives take a massive detour, turning upside down. In the prefrontal cortex, the decision-making stops and takes a backseat, whilst the limbic system drives the car.

When grieving the person minimises awareness of thoughts related to the loss, which results in heightened anxiety and inability to think rationally. What happens is that we forget how to think, talk, and feel. Some of my clients describe feeling as if they are having a stroke, fumbling for words, not recognising phone numbers, and forgetting where they live.

I would frequently lose things when I was feeling the loss, keys several times a day, I would forget who I was about to call, or even forget someone's name. It is widely understood that the more complex the grief, the more one will have cognitive decline.

The results of trauma on adults can manifest in many different ways, mental health disorders, interpersonal problems, low self-esteem, trust issues, addiction, self-destruction, the list can go on. My experience both personally and professionally is that not until the recovery starts do, we see the connection between the current issue and the history of the trauma.

Addiction is something I have not experienced personally, however, the number of children I have removed permanently from their parents because of addiction is staggering. Naively I used to think, that the risk of losing your child would be enough to conquer the addiction. I was naive to think that an addiction that is related to trauma could so easily be cured. Of course, losing their child to the care system would have been horrendous and traumatic for them, the addiction was likely made worse by the actions of removing their child and or threatening the removal.

Adults who are hiding, harbouring the deep-seated pain from the trauma are prone to using substances to help them cope and blackout the memory. Taking drugs or alcohol affects the way, you feel, both physically and mentally. The feelings from being drunk or on drugs can be enjoyable and escapism from the past.

What I realise now is trying to get a parent to stop using drugs or alcohol to keep their child in their care is ineffective because the cause of the addiction is not being managed and or solved, something that needs to be considered and re-assessed in social care.

The human brain is amazing and adapts to its environment. The brain adapts and responds to everything that happens in your life. Everything that takes place, good or bad causes the brain to change. It's because of this that whatever you may experience in your childhood is likely to follow you through your life, it shapes how to think, behave, and relate to the world.

When there is trauma this can cause the brain to have abnormalities in the brain structure, which can cause problems with behaviour and cognitive thought. High levels of cortisol which is a stress hormone in childhood impede the brain from normal development.

Punishment is generally considered an effective way to shape human behaviour, it is what our justice system is based upon. Truth be told, there is a subset of our population where this simply doesn't and cannot apply. Survivors of childhood trauma. Childhood trauma affects brain functioning, and those who have experienced extreme stress as children create adults who fundamentally are unable to correctly consider risk and make healthy life decisions.

Although it is widely documented that children who experience trauma are at risk of behavioural problems as they grow, the neurobiological processes that contribute to this are not understood. That is not to say poor behaviour, risky behaviour, illegal behaviour should not be challenged, of course, it must be to keep society safe, but what saddens me is that we have adults who have not had the correct recovery treatment so that they can learn new ways of functioning and behaviour tools, something I am trying to change.

I have spent my whole adult life in the field of child protection, and have been an expert witness for the courts many times, I have worked for many organisations within the safeguarding arena, and mostly they try their best to keep children safe, what there is little of is the early intervention, the changing cycle of abuse, the treatment required for adults and children so that they can be healthy.

I am working currently with a lady who had some difficult experiences at Church, it is no secret that the Church has a dark history when it comes to childhood abuse and trauma. The difficulty when there is trauma within a faith is that not only does the adult need to recover from the abuse, their faith is often removed from them also.

Only once have I had to leave an organisation because it was fundamentally flawed and unsafe, and that was the Church of England. My experience is much like other safeguarding professionals within it, that it refuses to acknowledge adequately the abuse of children and adults.

I have asked myself the question of why this happens, and can only hypothesise that they are scared of abuse, scared of talking about it, changing what is clearly ingrained within. I was so ashamed by the way the Church of England dealt with safeguarding I had no alternative but to leave after whistleblowing for months, even to this day, I am haunted by my experience, as I had used the church as a tool for my own recovery, and this experience almost wiped away all the good that Christianity had done for me before.

I do not mention this to bash the Church of England, the press does this enough already, I tell you this to explore that even big organisations can get it wrong when there is a lack of knowledge, understanding, and ignorance around trauma and its effects. Through education and training, organisations can I believe change, and together with a voice, we can do this. Part of my work is to go into these large organisations and talk to them about trauma, it must not be hidden, it must be brought into the light because until it is, we cannot help stop it.

Chapter 4

Healing the Traumatised Person Holistically

Holistic therapy is a form of healing that considers the person as a whole, healing their body, mind, spirit, and emotions, this will create optimal wellbeing and wellness. Part of the recovery is finding a proper balance in life whilst utilising the holistic approaches.

I believe that the whole person is made up of many different interlinking parts, and if one part is not working properly, the rest of the parts are affected. Therefore, should there be an imbalance in the physical, emotional, or spiritual parts, it will negatively affect the ultimate health of the person.

That is not to say that conventional medicine and health support doesn't have an appropriate place in society, of course, it does, what I try to explain to my clients is that there is also another form of health care and that is the holistic and alternative approach. When I work with clients, they will often initially still use conventional health care as well as alternative care. If someone suffers from bad headaches, having conventional pain relief is good, but I would also look at the potential factors that may be causing the headaches. Other health problems, diet, sleep habits, stress, personal problems. We would then plan the treatments that would include medication at the beginning to relieve the symptoms, but also modifications of lifestyle to help prevent the headaches from recurring.

The foundation of holistic healing is the belief that unconditional love and support is the most powerful healer and a person is uniquely responsible for their own recovery, health, and well-being.

My experience of what I have seen is that all people have innate powers to heal themselves. I don't look at a client as a disease, they are only a person, people who need to recover from trauma need support and a joined-up approach to address the problems in the person's life, we become a team and for me treating the cause is the only option for recovery.

As a holistic recovery coach, I use a variety of treatment techniques to help my clients take responsibility for their own well-being because I want them to achieve a full recovery and optimal health.

My experience is that suppressing your emotions only spares others from the discomfort of having to manage your feelings. If you do not release your emotions it can cause a lot of harm to you. Men can often explode in rages when they finally unleash their emotions and suffering long-term physical and psychological damage for not healthily managing their stress and trauma. Men are sadly taught to display fewer emotions, which is what leads to the explosions, but the list of physical symptoms in different parts of their body is extensive. Many people who hold in their emotions have problems with toilet movements, bad backs, shoulders, and headaches are to name a few.

The stress that comes from unresolved emotions and trauma can trigger your flight or fight response. Harvard

Medical School did research on this area and found that not releasing your emotions slowed digestion, resulting in gas, bloating, constipation, vomiting, and occasionally ulcers. But if the emotions are of deep sadness and shame the emotion which is buried can explode as anger, which can put you at increased risk of heart problems. That is because the anger and rage one feels when emotions are deeply repressed and hidden causes the stress hormones to be increased, this can give an explosion of energy, but this burst of energy can cause blood vessels to tighten as blood pressure increases, which in time will affect the heart physically not just emotionally.

Pain in the neck and head are often one of the most common physical symptoms of unresolved emotions and trauma. This is because the stress of holding emotions causes muscles in the jaw to tighten. My jaw used to be so tight I could not even open my mouth sometimes until the pain moved to my head and neck. Stop frowning was something I have heard too many times in my life, yes I used to frown a lot, well I had a lot of stress in my life. What I have learnt is the frown which is obviously due to supressed stress, reduces blood flow to the brain, which is why I likely suffered from horrendous headaches.

PTSD, an anxiety disorder I work a lot with, I have seen great improvements in people's mental health by using alternative therapies. Of course, not all people with PTSD react the same way to each treatment. Over the last few years, I have seen an increase in people with trauma disorders using complementary and alternative therapies.

People need to know why they want recovery from their trauma and what they expect from the process. The goal is the be able to face the reality of the trauma without getting stuck in the past, to reduce the symptoms that the trauma has caused, to be in the present not the past, your daily functioning improves, to take control of your emotions and internal power, and to gain the tools to reduce any relapse.

That all sounds like fairy-tale talk, but believe me it is possible with the right treatment and the right support.

Using a holistic approach to recovery from trauma allows you to accept effective transformation en route. Taking each new approach and gaining new light into your life. Each approach brings something different, which allows for a relaxed approach to recovery, not relying on just one method to heal you.

Holistic modalities approach the problem at its root and eliminate it instead of covering up the symptoms, which basically then wreak havoc because the problems continue. My approach is to look at the person as a whole, I recognise that a healthy mind cannot exist without a healthy body, which is why my approach is to treat both mind and body which provides a more comprehensive and complex strategy.

There is no doubt that to holistically recovery we must refer to having a healthy lifestyle. Having vibrant health and well-being are essential elements of success which is why part of my programme is looking at what goes into the body, and how the body moves as well as what is inside the mind and soul.

I want everyone to live their best lives, which for me is not just surviving, it's thriving. I don't want you to just be existing, I want you to dream big and reach those dreams. I will help you take care of yourself so that you can be your best, that is what becoming your very own phoenix is all about.

To do that, we need to align your body, mind, soul, and spirit with the greater whole for the good of you and all those around you. You become reborn, re-created, no longer just a survivor, in turn, you can have a positive impact on the world.

Your body is the only one you have, and to get healthy physically we do have to have a good balanced diet, a routine of exercise so that it is strong enough to hold you. Working on both the physical body and spiritual self we can work towards a true wholeness.

Becoming whole and recovering from trauma means you are creating a bright future with is a tremendous gift for yourself.

I found the key to holistic recovery is meditation done daily. This is shown to reduce stress and anxiety. There is significant evidence now in supporting mindfulness/meditation as a treatment approach for trauma. Mindfulness reverses deregulation of the brain that was caused by the trauma, it increases the prefrontal and hippocampal activity, which calms down the amygdala. There is evidence from scans that show that mindfulness meditation has increased the grey matter in the hippocampus and a decrease in the grey matter of the amygdala.

My experience of recovery started when I learnt how to ground myself, something I do most days even now. To be grounded or grounding yourself basically means staying connected to the present moment without getting lost in emotions and or thoughts. It is a process that means finding your inner roots, your connection to the earth.

There are different types of grounding, but the focus is the connection between you and the earth. Some people do this by walking barefoot, allowing their skin to touch the natural ground can give you the energy you require. Others lie on the ground; some submerse themselves in water. I personally don't do any of those approaches and I teach a more mediative approach to grounding which can be done anywhere and takes just a matter of minutes.

Although there is not a great deal of research yet into the benefits of grounding, I, however, have had people report improvements in their well-being. I definitely have seen improvements in anxiety and depression when people ground, chronic pain, and chronic fatigue I have also seen improvements with. When I have trouble sleeping, I use grounding which is always helpful for me.

The purpose of meditation, mindfulness, and grounding is that they are tools that equip you throughout your journey, they are tools you can call upon whenever needed, although of course, I use other approaches too in the recovery process, there are some like the above which are quick to learn, master and reuse when needed without anyone else's help.

Recovery is our main focus and goal for people who have experienced trauma. What recovery doesn't do is give anyone complete freedom from their past and trauma. Using holistic approaches, allows the person to gently recover and although the recovery will look differently to everyone, what we hope for is that everyone can live in the now without being overwhelmed by their trauma.

Before you start to recover you can often feel helplessness, and loss of power and control. Using holistic approaches at the speed needed for the induvial restores the safety and empowerment back to the person.

I went to a few talking therapists in my recovery, big mistake, they never worked. They didn't work because with each of them, they wanted me to discuss my trauma in detail, how can discussing what happened to me in detail be good for me. My view which is widely debated throughout the professional world is that revisiting traumatic memories in fact causes more harm. That doesn't mean, I don't believe that one should never talk about the trauma, one likely should, it's to the level of detail that I question. I also do not believe that talking about the past is the first place to start. Trauma recovery is a process that needs to be worked on over some time with specific steps.

My trauma affected my ability to have any self-compassion, it was important for my recovery that I learnt and nurtured myself compassion. I always felt that I was able to show compassion to others but not myself, what I learnt is that to be truly congruent one has to be able to do both.

It's important to me that whilst we use holistic methods of recovery, we create a trustworthy and authentic working relationship. This type of connection is crucial to healing. It's about showing kindness to yourself, which can be a foreign concept I know, self-compassion that incorporates meditation builds on the Buddhist practices of "Loving Kindness". Using these practices through mindful awareness, you learn to notice that your negative thoughts of self-blame and hostility start to gently turn to a more compassionate view.

Loving yourself and being kind is a key to holistic recovery, if you allow yourself to experience true loving-kindness as a real feeling, you can address difficulties more directly, learn from them and see what change can take place.

Forgiveness is the key to recovery. I believe that teaching forgiveness is important for children who have suffered trauma because the trauma will have compromised the child's emotional health. Teaching children how to forgive will allow them as adults to forge stable and meaningful relationships as adults without anger being present which will only cause division and discord.

There are senseless crimes that happen, I should never have been abused as I was, that is why cultivating forgiveness is important, without the ability to forgive the crime or trauma it can cause a wave of anger within that can alter the course of people's lives.

Forgiveness neutralises the hurt. I try to see at least something good in everyone, and yes that can be difficult, but it is possible. For me forgiveness allowed me to see my negative emotions and stress differently. Forgiveness is not about the perpetrator, it's about the victim. I refused to allow my perpetrators to have control over my life any longer, but with all the healing in the world if you cannot forgive what has happened to you, then you cannot remove the hurt. So, I forgave them, so that I could move on. Once I learnt about forgiveness, I had a light bulb moment, my life changed direction, I felt healthier inside, the darkness shifted, I was also able to forgive myself. I was kinder to myself; I was able to let go of some of my shortcomings and begin my new life.

With the holistic practises I have learnt over the last two decades and the countless clients from all over the world I have worked with I am passionate about recovery, and we all have the right to be healthy and happy and it can happen to you.

Chapter 5

NLP and Timeline Therapy

When I first heard about NLP, I didn't initially train in it to heal myself, I had no idea I needed help, I thought I had dealt with my life. Ignorance is sometimes bliss, but it's still ignorant and not helpful in the long run. I walked into the training which took place one weekend a month for nine months with the same group of people. It was doing the training, that I started to see myself, understand why certain things had happened in my life, why I felt things the way I did. It was the true start to my, self-discovery and healing. I got so much out of the training that once I became a practitioner, I went on to complete the master practitioner stage another nine months of one weekend a month. I spent two years eating, sleeping, drinking NLP, and I can honestly say it saved my life. It was not easy, it was the hardest thing I have ever done, my panic attacks got worse before they got better, I started to fall apart initially, I had no idea who I was and just what damage my childhood had caused me.

I met people on the course who would change my life, good and bad. Change comes at a price and sometimes change makes us do things that we would not have thought we could do, it also made me ugly sometimes, until I got through the darkness and walked into the light and now, I can say it was totally worth it.

I had to walk away from some people because for my recovery I needed to have around me only people who I could trust, and who would not be a negative influence on my recovery. That was really tough, people don't understand why you are walking away, they don't understand they are part of your damaging behaviour, it's not them it's me, that's right. This was my journey, my recovery, they were not to blame, but they also could not be in my future.

This happens to most people who successively recover from trauma, there will be people in your life who are not helping the journey, and it's OK that you need to part ways, what is important is that you find inner peace for you, inner calmness and joy.

So, as I said, my therapy journey to recovery started really with NLP.

So, what is NLP?

Neuro-Linguistic Programming NLP is the practice regarding our thinking, feelings, language, and behaviours. NLP is about how we form unique internal mental maps of the world by the way we filter and perceive information via our five senses.

What is the Neuro

We are all unique individuals we have our own filtering system for processing data. The first mental map of our world will be made up of internal images, sounds, tactile awareness, internal sensations, tastes, and smells. This is called the "First Access" in NLP.

What is the Linguistic

We create personal meaning to any information we receive from the outside world. We develop a second mental map by assigning language to the internal images, feelings, sounds, tastes, and smells, this recreates a conscious awareness of life. This is known as the “linguistic map”

What is programming

This is the behaviour response that happens as a result of thought filtering and linguistic map.

We all have the resources we need to make positive changes to our lives. Using NLP techniques are tools to help with these changes. New patterns of behaviour and NLP techniques allow you to become your own expert in your life.

For me, as I have previously mentioned talking about the incident or trauma I believe is ineffective and in fact, can cause further harm that’s why I love NLP. NLP can be content free; you don’t have to tell me what the problem is in any great detail.

As well as being content-free, experience shows that NLP also tends to be fast, typically resolving issues in several brief sessions, which will of course make it very cost-effective and much cheaper than traditional therapies.

NLP techniques provide us with ways of helping and dealing with emotional problems, I often see clients with anxiety, confidence issues, self-esteem problems, bereavement, or destructive relationships. It is also helpful for people who suffer from phobias and fears, weight, and healthier lifestyle choices also.

When I use NLP with clients, we will use modelling, modelling is very rewarding, exciting, and can be life-changing. As small children we used modelling all the time to learn skills, sadly, most of us lose access to this skill as we grow up. What I try to do is help people re-learn the skill.

The purpose of modelling is to find someone who does something really well, you then observe and imitate that person like you would have done if you were a child. The purpose is to capture patterns of excellence present in someone.

When working with someone who is demonstrating poor decision making, or behaviours that are less than helpful to them, modelling someone who does life differently changes their perceptive and therefore allows them to know there is a different way and it can be done.

I remember when I first came across modelling, it seemed so alien but once you choose to embrace it, magic truly begins to happen.

I use NLP because it tries to detect and then change the unconscious biases and or limitations we have. It works through the conscious use of language to bring about the changes required in people's thoughts and behaviours.

As a master practitioner, I can identify a person's preferred representational system otherwise known as PRS. I do this by listening to what people say, for example when someone says “I see your point”, that would signify a visual PRS, or “I hear your point” would signify an auditory PRS.

Once I have understood your PRS I can frame the right approach to our sessions.

Methods I use:

Anchoring: I teach you to turn sensory experiences into triggers for certain emotional states.

Rapport: I tune into you; I will match your physical behaviours to help improve our communication and response through empathy. For example, if you sit with your legs crossed and arms around yourself, I would sit the same, mirroring you.

Swish pattern: we will work through changing patterns of behaviour and thoughts to come to a preferred outcome.

Visual/kinaesthetic dissociation: We will remove negative thoughts and feelings from your trauma.

What all of that does is teach you methods basically of personal development by self-reflection, confidence-building, and better communication.

I was traumatised by the neglect I suffered which developed a traumatised response to my childhood, which meant I found relationships difficult due to the fear of being rejected. I didn't know that's why relationships were difficult for me, it was an automatic response, a somatic response because of the trauma which I stored in my mind and body. As this is learnt behaviour, I had to un-learn it.

NLP was a lifesaver for me, it's so useful in this arena. It helped me create a line of communication between me, my memories, my beliefs, and behaviours.

I know I believed I was not worth loving, thanks to my biological parents, and so I would self-sabotage my intimate relationships before I could get hurt by them. It was doing the NLP courses that allowed me to recognise this. I learnt how I developed these behaviours and beliefs, and why they were part of my life, which in turn I could then change.

In our session, we will learn to understand your mind, and we will reprogramme it to better serve you. We will look at the negative automatic responses and change them into something more positive. With me I let go of the belief that people would hurt me, I started to believe that people would and could love me, most importantly that I was worthy of being loved.

It doesn't really matter what the trauma is that people have experienced, all trauma creates a behaviour response that can be improved and changed. I believe sincerely that we all would benefit from knowing what our behaviours are from trauma so that we can replace them with behaviour that creates a healthier person.

Due to my life experiences, I have suffered from PTDS, an area I am passionate about for others. The Visual Kinaesthetic dissociation, otherwise known as VKD is a good tool for the treatment of PTSD.

What VKD does is, encourage a reprogramming of the psychological response to the trauma. We break the connection between the image of what happened and the feelings of what happened, which then removes the trigger behaviour.

This works because we have together created a safe environment, and I would guide you in reprocessing the event, this allows you to update your perspective on the trauma and we remove the fight, flight, freeze response, as it is no longer required.

Of course, we are all different and respond differently to treatments, therefore I never just plunge straight into methods we always test the theory first. We would pick a slightly unpleasant event and work with that first, on a scale of 1 to 10, we would pick something that is only a 1 or 2, I do this as a practice dummy run. I want you to recover from your trauma so finding the right approach is key.

We also use metaphors which is a linguistic process that we use to transfer the idea of one concept to another concept. Its about the unconscious influence. Metaphors influence people without us realising.

Using a metaphor takes the story away from the conscious level which turns off any critical thinking. Your subconscious however cannot determine time, so the metaphor can have an effect on the now. You create a parallel reality, an "as if" mode.

Hindsight is a wonderful gift; we have all thought we would have done something differently if we had known. Well, that makes sense doesn't it because we got that hindsight by making previous mistakes, so we learn from them this time around. If you always do what you have always done, you will always get what you have always got. It makes sense does it?!

Everyone does their best with the tools he or she has available at the time. We learn lessons through our mistakes, what NLP tries to do is awaken your hindsight by accepting the lessons with gratitude and asking ourselves what did we learn from it, it's only then we can grow and evolve.

To learn new things, that will often mean taking ourselves out of our comfort zone. Like me writing this book, completely out of my comfort zone, but I wanted to grow and learn, challenging myself to a new adventure, a new circle.

Another technique we use within NLP, is Time Line Therapy, TLT. TLT is a very powerful therapeutic process that evolved from NLP. It applies the process to the concept that we linearly store memories within the internal memory.

The process eliminates the painful attachment to the memories and or event. It also helps us to focus on what we can learn from the event and how we can use the learning in the future.

I was really sceptical about NLP and TLT, when I did undertake the TLT, it without a doubt produced a lifelong transformation, far quicker than any other therapy I had tried. TLT taught me to clear my limiting beliefs which were stopping me from having the life I wanted.

What TLT does Is help you to release the chains of emotions in one go. For example, if you suffer from anger issues, TLT will erase all anger from your past rather than the anger from just one incident. That's why I felt so good so quickly and the results have stayed with me to this day. The thing to remember is none of this removes the memory of a traumatic event, what NLP and TLT does is remove the negative emotion attached to that event. I can still remember the sexual abuse (although I try very hard not to think about it) but it is there, but what I do not have is any negative emotion about it. I can talk about it without upset, I can remember it without feeling sick, I have detached myself from the emotion of the acts that happened against me.

When there are negative emotions in one's mind, we then create limiting beliefs, which then stop us from moving forward in a healthy and content manner. I always believed I didn't deserve happiness, I was not good enough, I used to see myself as an untouchable, no one wanting to be around me, I hated myself truth be told. Just writing that about myself I horrid, I hate the thought that anyone who has experienced trauma may feel that way. Unresolved negative emotions as I have already mentioned in a previous chapter creates physical symptoms on the body and illnesses. How we perceive stress and respond to it, is influenced by our emotions which if our emotions are unresolved will affect how we manage the situation.

I have always meditated but since using NLP and TLT my meditation is greatly improved and enhanced because I no longer suffer from limiting beliefs and negative emotions.

Chapter 6

Using Hypnotherapy to Heal

Sometimes we pick a terrible therapist, and I've done that, it almost destroyed everything I had. Picking a therapist is so important, someone who is properly trained, not someone who is half-trained, that was my mistake. The mistake that took four years from my life until I was able to see the wood through the trees. I'm not sure if some therapists know they are not very good, mine was harmful, something even to this day I'm not comfortable talking about. I tell you this because that therapist literally could have ruined my whole life, and I learnt that the hard way that ensuring your therapist is the right one is vital. It's not just about the training and correct insurances, liabilities, etc it's also about them, do they make you feel safe and secure without crossing professional boundaries.

Don't get stressed about how to find the right recovery worker, therapist, coach, counsellor whatever word better suits you. Knowing what you want to gain from healing and doing a bit of research about different types of therapy meridians will put you in a good position of choosing someone who uses the meridian you want to use.

When the relationship is right between client and recovery worker/therapist the work can literally rewire the brain to create a much stronger, healthier person, and that's when you will see the magic happen and positive changes in your life. Hopefully, this book will give you a little insight into some of the different holistic approaches available and how they can work.

There are many different types of recovery support practices, this book names but a few, the ones I talk about are the ones I have personal experience with and the ones that form part of my phoenix project. There are others, and they are just as valid.

This chapter will talk about Hypnosis and how can it help heal trauma emotions.

Hypnosis what is it and how is it used?

Hypnosis is a trance-like state in which you experience increased suggestibility, concentration, and attention. A good description would be to state hypnosis is a state of focused attention. When you are in a hypnotic state you will often seem zoned out or sleepy, but you are in fact in a state of hyper-awareness.

Hypnosis is an excellent tool in my experiences for trauma and therapy, and it notably can reduce anxiety. There are different ways hypnosis can be done. You can use guided hypnosis, which will often be a pre-recorded set of instructions and music, YouTube has tons of them. Full hypnotherapy is what I practice, and I use it specifically to help with PTSD, anxiety, and depression. There is also self-hypnosis, which is done by the individual, you would guide yourself into a hypnotic state, this is usually for managing stressful situation or pain in my experience.

Hypnosis is totally holistic and natural whilst being incredibly powerful. Hypnosis is not just a stage trick by

Paul McKenna or complementary therapy. Trance plays an important role in humans and used correctly it can help facilitate incredible changes from within.

When I have had hypnosis has a method of recovery it helped leave my depression behind, as well as other emotional problems I had. I have also used it for pain relief for clients and help with addictions.

Hypnosis is both a psychological and physiological experience. This happens every time you go to sleep. When you are asleep your physical surroundings disappear, and you enter a state where anything is possible, who hasn't had a flying dream, or a dream where you are on another planet, or speaking a different language, anything and everything is possible.

We spend about 25% of our sleep time in a dream state, some people remember dreams easily, others don't, but they still happen. The dream state is known as REM, it's also called paradoxical sleep since our physiology and psychology are completely different than when we are not in REM.

When we are in REM we are inward and only limited by our imagination, that is all hypnosis is. When you are in a deep dream, you have no concept of reality, and are completely immersed within your own self-created reality, hypnosis feels the same.

The Greek god of sleep is where the name hypnosis comes from, but the reality is that during hypnosis you are reaching the levels of REM but whilst being awake. Commonly, rapid eye movement seen whilst dreaming will also be observed during hypnosis.

The purpose of dreaming is the brain's way of clearing itself from emotional arousal, it's therefore easy to see how hypnosis then can be good for clearing negative emotions from people. When you are asleep your body doesn't move, of course, it could be very dangerous if it did especially if you were dreaming about jumping for example, what happens is your body is inhibited which is known as catalepsy, this also occurs within hypnosis, yet another similarity between REM and hypnosis.

When you are under hypnosis, your attention is narrowed, making sure you are fully focused on yourself and your own mind, you will experience some form of catalepsy and your eyes will move side to side. I used to suffer terribly with headaches, and it was during a hypnosis session where the therapist I found out later, suggested catalepsy to me, this hypnotically induced catalepsy was then used as anaesthesia for my headaches. Incredible, this was a turning point for me with regards to my belief system around hypnosis.

You don't always have to be under a deep hypnotic state some everyday trances also have their uses.

An example of an everyday trance is driving. Sometimes we zone out whilst driving, get somewhere without realising how we did it, or don't remember how we got to our destination. This is our unconscious competence which allowed us to drive safely even though another part of our mind was off elsewhere.

I use hypnosis as a tool to help unlock negative emotions and release the trauma surrounding them. During hypnosis we are all more suggestible, we can assess ideas without fear or knee-jerk reactions of our conscious mind. Whist we are under hypnosis we feel a sense of calm which means we can approach ideas, situations differently, and integrated them more easily.

My experience personally and professionally is that hypnosis is more helpful to me when trying to overcome deeply programmed emotional distress.

Hypnosis only works because it's a natural state for humans. When we focus our attention, we can concentrate, learn, remember, none of this would be possible without the ability to go inwardly through trance.

The difficulty with focusing inward, we enter a trance-like state. When you suffer from depression you will spend a lot of time focusing inward, the more you worry the more depressed you become. This type of trance is not helpful. Phobias are when people become transfixed by whatever the phobia may be, all other parts of reality disappear whilst you are in the moment of phobic response.

PTDS, as you will now understand, is the main focus of my work with people, well who have PTSD will often have moments of regression back to the original trauma, they become transfixed, hypnotised to the memory.

My point in all of this is that there is a naturally occurring hypnotic state often working against the person. A trigger response can happen even with regards to the name of someone. For me, I use hypnosis to help people overcome and take control of their trauma and lives, and I want them to not only survive but to strive.

Firstly, we use hypnosis to clear away the emotional blockages, then we use it to engage new behaviours. This is done by the use of relaxation in which we can then apply hypnosis.

When I was using hypnosis for recovery, the therapist would help me find better ways of feeling and different behaviours which would be more beneficial to me, and it would help me feel better and happier. I guess she was working on both my physical and psychological self.

I had a client in his mid-thirties who had sexual problems. His initial belief was that there was a physical problem, but in fact, it was both a physical and a mental problem. The psychology around sex was impacting his physical ability to get an erection. We used hypnosis to influence the mind and the body, rather than just one or the other.

I had another client who suffered from terrible irritable bowel syndrome, but by using hypnosis as a treatment of the psychophysical self, she was able to get on top of her condition.

The fact is the body works to how the mind feels, if the mind is not feeling right the body will not work right. It's that simple, we cannot recover without working on both.

Hypnosis for me is now a way of life, I use it to enhance my life regularly.

Often when I initially use hypnosis on clients, they tell me they expected to feel totally "out of it" unconscious even, but that is not the reality, your conscious mind is always there, I am just able to crack into the parallel awareness. After sessions, people will often feel really relaxed, like they have experienced a lovely adventure, and feel wonderful. The thing I ensure to my clients is that throughout the process you are still aware of your thoughts and your surroundings, you will know where you are, your conscious mind will be observing whatever manifests within the session.

Hypnosis is safe, you are always in control of the session, and not at any point are you unconscious. There are no side effects unlike medication, and my experience is that everyone every time gets something out of each session. I use hypnosis as a tool to heal from emotional trauma because it's not intrusive, it's relaxing, and enjoyable to the client.

I have often been asked and asked the same question myself, can everyone be hypnotised. I was adamant it wouldn't work on me, there was no way someone was going to have control over me. Which of course is what I thought about hypnosis in my ignorance. Truth be told if you are of the view that it will not work and you are totally resistant then it is likely that it would be difficult for you to relax enough to enter a deep trance. I had that view because I was adamant, I wouldn't release control, I learnt the hard way.

You never give up control of either your mind or your body, you do allow yourself to be deeply relaxed which allows your subconscious to do the work required to heal. This can only happen if the client trusts the therapist and you want to have hypnosis.

Chapter 7

How Does Coaching Help You Change?

Coaching is something I came across later in life, I started coaching whilst I was a social work manager and decided I would train to be a coach at work and then went in to change management coaching, to eventually be a trainer to the trainers in coaching. The thing I realised pretty quickly was the techniques could without a doubt be used within a therapeutic environment. I don't recommend coaching as the only tool to use for trauma, I use it at a later stage when the emotional work is being managed and we are looking to the future.

I have the great privilege to know a few coaches personally who are friends of mine, and each of them brings something different to the table. That's the thing about coaching, there are so many different approaches and avenues, there is someone our there for everybody. Coaching is a beautiful tool for personal transformation and growth. We are always growing and evolving, having a coach to hold your hand unconditionally through some of those changes is magical. This book is the result of a fabulous coaching friend of mine, who whilst we were talking, she started to ask me questions about my direction and where I was going, what I wanted, etc etc, well from there the realisation that the book I have been dreaming of writing although would take me out of my comfort zone was ready to be written and I could no longer keep making excuses for writing it, it was now or never.

Let's talk about coaching then. Coaching is about bridging the gap between where you are now, to where you would like to be, and how to get there with the support and direction of a coach, therefore not leaving you to do it alone.

It is a conversation that takes place between two people, or in groups. The aim is to make things happen and change. Often working out what patterns, beliefs or dynamics may be holding you from reaching those desired goals.

Being yourself, relationships, values, your core identity, needs, tasks, skills are the things a coach will deal with. It's all about empowerment through self-awareness. It is a collaborative process with the coach and client being equals and draws on innate strengths and resources.

As I have mentioned before the quality of the relationship between the coach and client is vital. Sessions can be structured, directional, there may be a specific model being used. The coach is there to help facilitate you doing quality thinking. The sessions are conversational but do also involve writing sometimes, there is always homework, all in all, it can feel daunting and challenging, but the coach is there to be unconditional and non-judgemental throughout the journey.

Coaching without a doubt changes people's lives and direction, and allows people to attain growth. A good coach is an expert in helping guide their client with great questions, they can help people enhance their full potential, overcome roadblocks, and create sustainable success.

The Process:

Before each session, I give my clients a quick questionnaire, this is a short list of questions that allows us to see any progress and success since the last session. It will also recognise any roadblocks and what's not happening easily.

This also allows the client to help focus and prepare for the session, the questionnaire is sent back to me before the session, therefore, allowing me to ensure the session will be adjusted to the client's needs

SMART plans, I have spent my whole social work career writing and managing SMART plans.

Specific, **M**easurable, **A**ttainable, **R**elevant, and **T**ime-based.

The purpose of a SMART plan is a clear structure with goals and time frames. Each goal comes with its own variable elements and no vague resolutions.

An example of that may be: I want to expand my business. To make it SMART the goal could be, I will get five new clients within my business within the next six weeks, by making two blog articles social media networking, and asking for referrals. This will allow the business to grow and thrive.

Each session I ask my clients to share 'gold nuggets' from the session. This allows them to see they had value from the coaching, this also helps clients have 'Aha' moments. I share all these gold nuggets and aha moments with the client throughout our time together.

Open-ended questions are the backbone to coaching, that's because they permit people to include more information, some examples of what you could expect me to ask.

What made you laugh today?

What are the most challenging things about being a member of your family?

What is your biggest fear?

Which accomplishment are you most proud of?

This allows me to better access your true thoughts and feelings on a topic, therefore I can direct our session accordingly.

Once something is down on paper, a goal, dream, aspiration, that is the first step of making it a reality. When I decided to get a coach and work through some stuff I needed to change, writing it down was cathartic, especially because I shared them with my coach and they were documented. It is a good tool also for expressing feelings and thoughts, as well as being able to keep a record of milestones made.

I find that writing enhances my power to focus during a change process and or new development. For people who suffer from depression, regular writing is linked to improved mood and reduction in stress levels.

I've never been very good at writing, I always wanted to keep a journal/diary sort of thing when I was younger, but I was terrified someone might read it and then know my darkest thoughts.

Today it's easier to keep things personal because of the internet and electronics so I do recommend writing to my clients, it's important to coaching when you are looking to achieve changes in one's self and one's life, that a reflection journal is made and updated with your emotions, observations, experiences, any challenges. And this can be written whenever you feel the need or want to rather than waiting for our sessions.

When I'm in a session, I am always fully there. I take a few minutes before each session to ground myself and prepare to be ready and open for you. It's important to my clients that I am listening and watching them throughout, so out of joint respect, there is no technology in our sessions in regards to mobile phones, etc.

Feedback between sessions is important, I want my clients to know I am there to hold their hand through the change, and requesting feedback between sessions allows them to know I am interested. This also helps me, because I can prepare for sessions and make sure they are meeting your needs and goals as I know where you are at throughout.

Homework is essential in coaching, the purpose is to keep you on track whilst we are not in sessions, they allow you to reflect, and take what action is required. It also helps you see if your plans are being achieved. You have the responsibility to make the changes happen, and homework makes the coaching a reality in real life and not just in our sessions.

We then move onto the grow model, which is a goal-setting with problem-solving.

G-Goal, what do you want to accomplish

R-Reality, what is the current situation, the current status quo

O- Obstacles, what is in the way and how we overcome them

W-Way forward, actions need to be put in place.

Once I had done the hard work of recovery from my trauma and spent time healing, I was ready to have coaching for my future. I needed someone to help guide me in how to get to where I wanted to get, career, family, and health, and I am very happy I decided to invest in myself, I deserved it, you deserve it never forget that.

Chapter 8

Energy Healing

When I was working through the pain of my past, I needed to find a place where I felt held, a place I could be vulnerable safely, somewhere I could feel peace and quiet within. It was whilst I was exploring avenues, I came across energy healing. Reiki, quantum touch, EFT, and hands-on healing most specifically.

Faith is something I usually keep to myself, but throughout my life, I have leaned on God. When I was six, I would take myself to church on a Sunday whilst my foster family did not go. They were Pagans and did not attend church. I don't know why I went to church, let alone by myself, but the need was there. I always felt comfortable when I was around the nuns, I felt safe, one nun used to often put her hand on my shoulder and say she was sending me Gods love. I now understand that to be laying on of hands. I have undertaken different energy healing training and with each of them, the course leaders have always said we are open to using whichever God or Life Source you feel aligned to when asking for healing through the hands. This is disputed by some orthodox believers of the faith, but I just don't think it matters. I take my energy from the Angels and God, that's where I believe my healing ability comes from. If someone doesn't believe that, then that is also OK. What's important is that the people being healed feel good through the process and no harm is done.

Having healing is a gift, and when you are working so hard to recover from your trauma, allowing someone to boost your soul with love and peace is beautiful. It's giving you something back, replenishing your energy.

Quantum-Touch is a method of natural energy healing that works with the life force energy of the body which promotes optimal wellness. Quantum-Touch makes us focus and direct the energy which benefits throughout the body. It's based on love, and the love you give to someone through your healing hands has a tremendous impact on those around you.

Energy healing is about how the practitioner channels the life force energy to accelerate the natural healing process.

We use that energy to remove blocks within the body and stimulate the body's ability to heal itself. We do this by balancing your energy which in turn improves your overall well-being.

Quantum-Touch gets to the root cause of a problem and creates space for the body to heal, it's called body intelligence, the belief is the body knows how to heal itself it just needs direction.

I work with a lady who has chronic autoimmune conditions, and this causes her high levels of pain, and we have sessions directly for her pain which diminishes once the session is over without her needed to take conventional pain relief.

Although I am directing the energy and helping your body consume it, you are the healer, not me, all healing is self-healing.

Reiki another meridian I utilise is a Japanese technique for the reduction of stress and helps promote relaxation. It is a further "laying on hands" process, and again like Quantum-Touch, it's all about directing the life force energy.

If our energy is low, then we are likely to start to feel unwell and stressed, although when our energy is raised, we feel happy and healthy.

I worked with a man who was bullied at work and had time off due to feeling depressed as a result. He would often state he had no energy, and felt all consumed by his negative emotions from the workplace. His stress levels had got so high, he was forgetting things, losing items, not sleeping. He was going through trauma from the bullying. We did some hypnotherapy and timeline therapy to break the emotional connection to the bullying, and we then used Reiki to increase his energy level. Using the combination of all three resulted in him being able to return to work, he felt more in control of his mind and his body was no longer feeling weak.

Depending on your religious beliefs if any, reiki is made up of two words Rei which means God's wisdom, and Ki which is life force energy. So whichever spiritual path you take, Reiki is a spiritually guided life force energy.

When I give someone Reiki my clients will often say that they feel the flow of energy through them and around them, the whole point of energy healing is that it heals the body, emotions, mind, and spirit.

It's a totally natural form of healing and self-improvement, that is available to everyone, I've always had a positive outcome and it does not interrupt other medical interventions.

Although Reiki is a spiritual tool, it is not a religion, it has no dogma and there is nothing you must believe to learn or use Reiki.

When I give someone Reiki it should be done in a peaceful setting, it can be online, or in person. All you need to do is be able to sit on a comfortable chair or lie down, we will often have relaxing music. When face to face I use the hands-on approach although when doing it online I send the energy rather than touch the person.

A method I have created is what I call the Hypno-Heal. I put my clients into a mild hypnotic relaxed state, and then give them energy healing. I find that because people are in a trance, they can absorb the healing on a subconscious level and often with a deeper and more profound result.

I believe the body can in the right circumstances, heal anything. I was working with an elderly lady who had stage 3b bowel cancer, she had the tumour removed and cancer had spread to five lymph nodes. She decided given her age and vulnerability at the time that chemotherapy was not an option for her. She would in her words "take my chances" the doctors told her the likeness is that the cancer will spread further without treatment.

I started to give her energy healing not to cure the cancer but to help her body recover from the surgery and allow her some R&R time, she needed it. We continued to have regular healing sessions using my Hypno-Heal method, and two and a half years later the cancer has not spread from the lymph nodes something the doctors have been astounded with. Now, this could be coincidental, but she believes it's her body utilising the energy to heal and repair itself and who am I to say it isn't. that's the magic of energy healing.

Emotional Freedom Technique or EFT is a tapping healing. EFT operates on the premise that if there is a physical problem with your health, there will be an emotional blockage that causes physical ill-health.

Even though tapping can be used directly to physical ill health, my experience is that getting to the root cause of the problem will likely result in a more long-term benefit.

The foundations of EFT believe that the more emotional trauma you release and heal from, the more peace and emotional freedom you will have in your life. Bearing that in mind, EFT is a good tool to help clear out old traumas and welcome a healthy and happy attitude.

EFT combines the physical benefit of acupuncture with the cognitive benefits of conventional therapy for a complete treatment of emotional issues and physical health.

Although EFT is related to acupuncture, it does not use needles, it stimulates certain meridian points on the body by tapping on them with our fingertips. It balances the disturbances in the meridian system, it is a therapy that can be done anywhere by anyone. Once you have learnt where the points are and how to tap you can do it yourself.

What's beautiful about EFT is the discovery statement.

"*The cause of all negative emotions is a disruption in the body's energy system*"

Now what that statement does not say is that the negative emotion is caused by a previous trauma, in other therapy practices they like to treat the memory, asking the client to relive their trauma, something I have already previously said I disagree with for trauma treatment and EFT treats the effect without reliving the trauma.

So let's recap on what the benefits are of energy healing whichever type of meridian you chose.

After a session you will feel lighter, you will notice this difference. As negative energy leaves your body and fresh new energy enters, the energy starts work on your cells straight away, supporting your body and mind.

Your subconscious thoughts that create blocks are released by the healing, allowing you to create new possibilities.

The most important element of healing is the release of emotional trauma associated with past experiences, that's because the trauma itself is held within the subconscious mind and the healing can enter the subconscious mind.

Some of our problems within the body come from ancestral programming, good energy healing can release these setting you free.

We are energy beings and life is made up of energy, because everything is energy we have energetic ties to everything, healing can release and uncut these ties.

Once the negative energy has been released, we can create new beliefs about ourselves and take control of our futures.

The transformation then takes place, this will happen after just one session, but with a programme of sessions, you can create true transformation.

Ultimately healing is up to you, it's your journey to take, the healer is just there to help facilitate the changes required.

Chapter 9

Meditation and Manifestation

Before I begin to discuss meditation, I have always spent time in my head, I have talked previously about attending church, so prayer and being quiet was something I had already spent my life doing. However, prayer alone for me was not enough and when I started to work through my issues I needed to find an additional avenue for my inner self to find peace. and finding something that would almost create a new home for my inner self. That's when I came across meditation.

Meditation is a technique that is intended to encourage a heightened state of awareness and attention.

- Meditation has been practiced in cultures all over the world.
- Every religion has a tradition of using meditative practices.
- You don't have to have a religious belief to use meditation.
- There are several different forms of meditation.

Meditation alters a person's conscious awareness which has a positive impact on your health both physical and emotional, I didn't know until I started to meditate, that it could impact and help physical ailments.

I use meditation for reasons now.

Stress, headaches, back pain, anxiety, self-awareness, gaining a better level of empathy with myself, and improvements with mindfulness.

It's easy to start meditating, once you have decided you want to try, find a quiet spot where there will be no distraction, maybe start with a short time limit of ten minutes, focus on your breathing taking deep breaths, and then take notice of your thoughts. The purpose of meditation is not to clear your mind, your mind will wander it's inevitable, just keep bringing your attention back to your breath, don't worry about your thoughts, and don't judge them.

Meditation can take different forms; I use two forms usually, concentrative meditation and mindfulness meditation.

Concentrative meditation involves focusing all of your attention on a specific object while tuning out everything else around you. The goal is to really experience whatever you are focusing on, whether it's your breath, a specific word, or a mantra, to reach a higher state of being.

Mindfulness meditation includes, among others, both mindfulness-based stress reduction and mindfulness-based cognitive therapy. Mindfulness can target different issues, such as depression, which means that its focus may be different from practice to practice. Overall, it involves the state of being aware of and involved in the present moment and making yourself open, aware, and accepting.

I have gained so much from meditation both psychologically and physically. I used to suffer from panic attacks and anxiety, which is better managed now through meditation, my clients use it as a tool for stress management and improved emotional well-being.

When I was in the process of whistleblowing about the church and eventually left, someone within the church wrote some things about me that were so incredibly disrespectful and ugly, my anxiety got dramatically worse as a result. I couldn't even leave my house alone. The thing about any trauma is sometimes when you are experiencing something, you are so 'in it' that you can't actually think about what is best for yourself on that day.

Even now when my stress levels reach fever pitch it can take me a while to realise what is needed, and or someone talking to me about it. The bonus of working in my field is I'm surrounded by experts who are now my friends, and I get free advice sometimes when I'm least looking for it, but gosh does it help. It was meditation that helped me work through my anxiety caused by the church, and although the meditation doesn't remove what has happened, it affords me the capacity to manage my feelings, and in turn that allows me to move on.

Meditation is about the deliberate means to change the course of your conscious thinking, which in turn alters how you perceive and respond to the world around you.

Meditation makes you feel happier, that's because it causes the pituitary gland in our brains to release endorphins that help our moods because it alters the brain activity it enhances our emotional experiences.

Meditation reduces stress, the endorphins that are released act as a stress stabiliser to the brain allowing you to stop worrying about the small stuff and concentrate on the big stuff. This was completely true for me, meditation removes the stress of the little stuff.

Meditation helps you focus, it is a disciplined method of healing, allowing you to focus on specific tasks which will increase efficiency.
Sleep is enhanced by quality meditation that's because whilst you are meditating you are focussing the mind which will aid relaxation.

I have had many clients confirm a reduction in pain especially those who suffer from chronic pain, once they create a standard meditation routine with it being regular.

My experience of meditation is that the more I meditated the better I connected to people, my compassion for people was more focused, and after meditation, I am always left with a greater level of love for people in general, which can never be a bad thing right?

The thing about meditation is the more I do it, the more people appear to want to be around me. It's as if it causes people to gravitate towards the positivity I am exuding from my meditation.

All these benefits make you ultimately healthier and happier with yourself and your life. I have found that meditation is often overlooked as a method of healing but anything that helps you feel happier and better must be a good thing.

Manifestation

I first read the book "***The Secret***" in 2006, some 14 years ago now, the film if you have not watched it, is currently on Netflix and I highly recommend it to you all. It's all about manifestation and the law of attraction.

Manifestation is the art of bringing tangible change into your life through belief and sheer optimism.

It is the mind that charts the course of how you will live. It is the heart that offers the deepest yearnings for what you must do.

The understanding that you live within, and learning how to manifest is much easier than you think.

At its root, manifesting is the practice that precisely helps you access your inner ability to create the life you want.

When you think something and believe it in, that determines what you perceive. Your mind is needing clues in life that then validate your reality, so the principle is that when you open up to what you want, you open your mind to clues that will lead you to what you want. Simple right?

If we are to believe this theory and why not, seems to be a great theory to believe in. Then this book has come to you for a specific reason, you asked for it, there is something in this book that you needed to hear. I would love to have any feedback regarding that comment, once you have finished reading my book, was there something you needed to hear in my book. I bet there was. You manifested this book to cross your path because you need it.

If we remove the ego out of the vision of manifestation, the process itself is simple. We chose to live as we do, and as we embrace a better state of awareness, we start to feel a power grow within us, that power is intentional, positive, and manifestation.

So how do we do it, how do we make a dream the reality, seemingly out of thin air? It's all about the Law of Attraction. There are eight principles of manifestation which can be started today.

You have to believe in yourself, and although this can be difficult, it is in your hands, your choice, if you struggle with believing in yourself, play the pretend game, the what-if game. What would it look like if I did believe in myself, visualise yourself believing in yourself? Acknowledge you are capable of self-belief. You want a better life to allow that thought you have built within you.

You need to have a plan, write it down, read it, own it, knowing that what it is you want is waiting for you. It's there for you to have.

start to take action, write your goals, meditate on them, stay active, tell yourself and everyone else what you intend to accomplish, write a journal daily. I told people about this book before it was finished because I knew that once I had said it out loud to other people I had no choice, I had to complete it.

keep positive thoughts going, positive vibrations attract positive vibrations. Negative feelings and emotions dilute your vibration. Imagine you are full of love, happiness, peace, and only let the light in, bright energy this will help to amplify your vibration.

Visualise what it is you want, visualise you having it

Always stay grateful and humble.

Having gratitude and feeling blessed daily will help the process move forward. Be thankful for the universe and yourself.

There are other ways to manifest, "The 369 Method", which Is basically writing it down 3 times, then 6 times, then 9 times every day for at least 40 days whilst meditating about it and visualising it.

Ultimately, it's all about the power of your mind to believe you can, then you will do so.

I am going to put it to the test with this book.

I believe this book will be a top bestseller. I will use the 369 methods; I will do it every day until the end of January when I will publish the book.

Chapter 10

Decluttering Your Home

I have not yet had a client who was needing to work on their trauma recovery who didn't need help with some form of de-cluttering either in their home, office or even car. I kid you not, I have known several people whose car was so full of things that they could never take passengers.

Trauma triggers the brain to function differently, trauma causes people to have difficulty making decisions, which is a classic reason why people often have a cluttered environment.

I have many clients who are surrounded with clutter and they say they feel out of control, they blame themselves, they often believe there is something wrong with them.

The first thing we do is assess how much stuff you have, do you have too much stuff. This might seem an obvious question, but it could just be that there is a problem with finding a place for stuff. Is your wardrobe overflowing and yet you can't find anything to wear, do you like a good bargain, or do you have emotional attachments to things that you don't want to get rid of.

You might think that the easiest solution is to just grab boxes and organise it all. You can't organise excess stuff. We try and ask people to get rid of 10 items a day, if the item is something you are attached to but you don't have room for it, look for creative ways to keep the memory alive without keeping the item.

When we work with someone around de-cluttering there are two important questions we ask:

1. **Do you use the item regularly?**

When was the last time you used it? Unless the item is something you only use for a specific season or event, if you haven't used it in the last six months, you probably don't need it. If you can't remember the last time you used it, let it go.

Your home should only hold things you use regularly. If there comes a time when you need a rarely used item, more often than not, you can find a suitable alternative or borrow it from someone else.

2. **Do you love this item?**

Honestly assess your item. Does it evoke positive or negative emotions for you? Does it make you happy? If the emotion it brings up for you is not a positive one, it does not deserve to be in your home. If it makes you feel guilty, sad, inadequate, etc. it most likely isn't something you need or want in your home.

There are great reasons to take on the task of de-cluttering.

Firstly you will have more space, having loads of stuff in your space is often an obstacle of distraction from your feelings and thoughts. If you start to de-clutter the area will feel more spacious, which will give your brain more space and that's because the stuff you see are visual cues that prompt memories, guilt, stress, etc.

You will appreciate what you have, when you start to think more clearly about what you choose to have around you in the home, you will become more selective, which will, in turn, allow you to appreciate what you have. When there is less stuff around you, you will have the space to spend more time on your own self-care.

You will learn what it is you really like, a lot of stuff you have I am sure are things you don't even like anymore, but until you start to go through all your stuff, you won't know. The thing you liked twenty years ago will likely be different now, de-cluttering will let you see how your tastes have transformed.

Once you get into the process of de-cluttering, you won't keep buying stuff because it was on sale, therefore saving you money.

You can make money too because as you go through stuff, you will find items that you can sell. Quid's in!

Also, on the money front, if you are wanting to sell your house, potential buyers will be put off if they see too much stuff in the house, a de-cluttered home looks and feels bigger.

Once the area is de-cluttered it will be easier to keep clean and you may feel more inclined to invite friends round, finally allow you to live a freer life.

We can do the theory with you online during our virtual sessions if that's how we are doing sessions, but I do recommend you have someone present who can help you actually go through the stuff and remove them out of the space.

Sometimes, you may think you are ready to embark on de-cluttering, but the reality is, that sometimes it is not the right time. One of my consultants and I were working with an 80-year-old woman, and she wanted to go through her loft.

Her house we could always tell for full to capacity and therefore likelihood was the loft was as full. We were not wrong, but it became apparent within the first session that she was not ready.

She found the process too traumatic, even trying to remove 40-year old wrapping paper was too much for her. I am always honest with my clients about expectations and the process. It wasn't right for her to clear the loft, it wasn't right for her at that time to clear her home, and that is also OK.

Safety is paramount, of course, if we find a situation that places a person at significant risk of harm due to the amount of stuff then we would need to consider other alternative options.

Chapter 11

The Phoenix Package

Now you have read my journey, how I did it, and what was involved.

Are you ready to take charge of your life? Are you ready to finally recover from the trauma that happened to you?

Are you ready to embrace the new you?

If you answered yes then ***You are the Phoenix*** is the place to come to.

You are the Phoenix is a one-stop-shop for holistic trauma healing. There are so many different treatment options and types of therapy out there, that quite frankly it's a mine field and that's how the phoenix package was started, I had a few clients who would come to me asking for a specific therapy type, which we would start and then it would become clear that actually, another meridian would also benefit them.

I have spent twenty years training in many different holistic therapies not to be a therapist, but to heal myself. I got something from all of them, healing from trauma is not easy, there is no quick easy fix, and what I have learnt is that the journey takes time, and as we grow and evolve our needs change, what help we need differs and that how you are the phoenix can help.

Trauma is something I would not wish upon anyone, it can literally ruin your life and freeze you at that moment in time. I believe that everybody deserves the best care in order to make them the best version of themselves, hence become their very own Phoenix, rising from ashes, leaving behind the old trauma, and flying high with new strength and power.

My life was pretty messed up, I made stupid decisions, I reacted to events inappropriately, I had unsafe and unhealthy relationships, I suffered eating disorders, I would self-harm, all because I had no idea that my trauma had caused my brain to function differently, my ability to regulate emotions, was off-key, my emotional growth had been stilted and none of that was my fault, but I still was the one in the driving seat of my life and could not allow my past any longer to hold my future back. So if I could do it, you can do it, and you have me holding your hand throughout the process.

The package is a six-month programme of self-discovery and recovery. Our packages are bespoke to you, we go through what you feel you struggle with and come out with a plan that best meets your needs. We use all the therapies that I have written about, each one of them has its place in trauma recovery. You may have picked up that the therapies are all gentle, and nurturing to your soul. Your soul is what needs to be nurtured and loved unconditionally, and that is what we teach you to do.

I have clients all over the world, and most of our work is done virtually and or face to face if we can make that happen. Sometimes I may suggest however, you find a practitioner of a specific therapy close by to you if I feel it's in your best interest.

On top of the therapies that we offer, part of the package is also about your physical self-care. I have consultants who work with me, some of the best in the world I have come across in their fields.

You will have a session with a personal trainer, they will look at what you eat and how much you move, it's important that when you commit to recovery that your body is strong for you, eating, exercise and living a clean life is vital.

You also have the opportunity to meet with a clothing coach, she will go through your clothing style, what colours are best on you, and then walk you through your wardrobe, she is a fully qualified coach who specialises in making people look amazing. There is no doubt that when take care of yourself, and look good, you feel better.

Finally, you have the option to meet with a de-clutter specialist, again this can be virtual but sometimes help within the house would also benefit that process.

By the end of the six months, you should feel like you are en route to becoming the phoenix. Your past and trauma will no longer control your life, you wont forget what happened to you, but truth be told would you actually want to? but you will be able to have the life you wanted.

The programme can be completely virtual, so wherever in the world you are, we can make it work for you, the power of positive thinking and the internet.

Chapter 12

Where I Am Now

Today I write this book after spending decades trying to recover from my childhood, and I made it, probably the best anyone can. I'm not perfect by any means and still have bad days where the emotions take over me and I go into the "flight" mode. There will always be certain situations that take me back, but on the whole, I do pretty well.

Now I am an author, a holistic trauma coach, inspirational speaker, and my greatest achievement and joy is that I am a mother and wife.

Being a parent was the big test for me, would I make it, could I do it, what if I ruin their lives. My journey to self-discovery and recovery was cemented on the birth of my daughter. It was now or never, I had to make good from all those techniques and put into practice all that I had learnt.

I was terrified to be a parent, I didn't want to turn out as my biological parents had, I didn't want to ruin my children's lives, it did create a wave of anger in me and frustration that decades after being removed from them, they could at some level interfere with my thoughts.

Being angry and sad about what my birth parents did to me and let happen to me, would have made me a terrible mother if I had kept hold of the negative emotions. I refused to allow them to ruin my ability to be a good mum. They had already taken away my childhood and impacted my early adulthood, I was not going to allow them to take away any more of my future. I had to forgive them. Forgiveness was not for them, forgiveness was for me, my soul, and my heart. Forgiveness gave me the control back, gave me the ability to put what happened in a box, and place it where I could reach if needed. Of course, forgiveness is the most difficult task of all, but with the NLP, hypnosis, and all the energy healing on top of meditating and manifesting what I wanted, it could be done. I did it. I have no ill will towards them, I still even think of them from time to time, because of the invention of the internet I have been able to keep an eye on them in fact. I'm not sure why I do, it gives me some comfort just knowing they are out there and not dead. I dread if I'm honest when they die, how am I meant to feel?

On the whole, I now live a peaceful life, material stuff means little. My husband laughs at me because I could move to a new house or country with one suitcase per person, people, that's what matters. Kindness, love, joy, and personal acceptance are what we hold inside, not what we place on the mantlepiece.

Probably because I had very little as a child, I have felt I have not needed much even now. I know people who had similar childhoods but are completely the opposite, they have so much stuff they don't know what to do with it. We all carry our scars differently.

I am the eldest child of 10, almost all of us were adopted out. I have no meaningful relationship with my birth siblings except one brother. It's hard because when you do not grow up with someone and yet they are your biological family, finding the balance is tough. I don't even know the names of several of my siblings, its very strange to know there are so many other people out there related to me somewhere, anywhere, nowhere who knows.

This is a burden I have had to get used to living with. This was one of the most difficult and emotionally harmful parts of my journey. In social work today, social workers try everything to keep siblings together, or at least to ensure they keep contact. If I could have changed any one thing from my childhood, it would have been that. I missed out on being a sister, I missed out on knowing my siblings, sharing a bond, allowing our children to then have a bond with one another. It's all just very sad.

When I was 19, I did try and fight for contact with my siblings I knew about, but the adoptive parents didn't want me in "*their children's*" lives.

I'm not sure if my siblings have been impacted by the decision made for us all those years ago, but I can honestly say I believe it was the cruellest decision the "*experts and new parents*" made on our behalf.

I do have a wonderful foster sister who I lived with between 5 to 10 and really, she is my sister in my heart. I'm so grateful for her because she understands what is like being in care and being adopted and have not great relationships with your biological family.

That's the thing about siblings they share experiences, parenting styles, stories of growing up together, I have that with her, and our children are all cousins.

Finally, and likely the most important thing about me is that I am happy.

I do have a wondering soul for sure, my dream is to pack the kids into the back of a campervan and travel the world together living off-grid whilst working remotely in helping other people find their voice and inner self. Today is not the right time for us, but we will when it is right to do it, embark on our biggest adventure together.

Printed in Great Britain
by Amazon

61694332R00058